Ministry By Objectives

by

Daniel L. Mead and Darrel J. Allen
Mead & Allen Consultants
Plainwell, Michigan

EVANGELICAL TEACHER TRAINING ASSOCIATION
110 Bridge Street • Box 327
Wheaton, Illinois 60187

Books in Evangelical Leadership Preparation series:

Christian Education Thru Music
Ministry By Objectives
Tips for Teaching Adults
Let's Talk About Teaching
Teach With Confidence

First Edition
First Printing 1978

Library of Congress catalog card number: 78-59182
ISBN 0-910566-84-4
© 1978 by Evangelical Teacher Training Association
Printed in U.S.A.

Scripture quotations are from the New American Standard Bible, ©The Lockman Foundation 1960, 1962, 1963, 1968, 1971, 1972, 1973, 1975, and are used by permission.

Quotations for *Organization and Leadership in the Local Church* by Kenneth Kilinski and Jerry Wofford. © 1973 by The Zondervan Corporation. Used by permission.

Contents

Foreword / 5

Preface / 7

Introduction / 9

1. Appraise the Situation / 11

2. Define the Work / 23

3. Develop Objectives / 33

4. Plan Strategy / 45

5. Execute the Plan / 55

6. Review and Revise / 69

A Final Word / 79

Practical Management Activities

Prac-tivity 1	/	13	Prac-tivity 13	/	53
Prac-tivity 2	/	16	Prac-tivity 14	/	53
Prac-tivity 3	/	18	Prac-tivity 15	/	58
Prac-tivity 4	/	26	Prac-tivity 16	/	59
Prac-tivity 5	/	26	Prac-tivity 17	/	60
Prac-tivity 6	/	28	Prac-tivity 18	/	60
Prac-tivity 7	/	42	Prac-tivity 19	/	64
Prac-tivity 8	/	43	Prac-tivity 20	/	65
Prac-tivity 9	/	50	Prac-tivity 21	/	71
Prac-tivity 10	/	50	Prac-tivity 22	/	75
Prac-tivity 11	/	51	Prac-tivity 23	/	76
Prac-tivity 12	/	52	Prac-tivity 24	/	77

Index to Supplemental Materials

Lay Worker Time Evaluation Guide / 14
Pastor's Time Evaluation Guide / 15
Work Evaluation Chart / 17
Organization Survey / 20
Weekly Church Activities Diary / 22
Church Organizational Chart / 27
Lay Leader Position Description / 30
Vocational Worker Position Description / 32
Formulating Objectives—Top-Down Process / 36
Formulating Objectives—Base-Up Process / 38
Goal Setting and Evaluation / 46
Christian Service Survey / 57
Monthly Ministry Report / 62
Monthly Report for Group Activity Leaders / 63
Sunday School Superintendent
   Performance Covenant / 67
Self-Evaluation Work Sheet / 72

Foreword

My first contact with Ministry By Objectives was through Sunday school superintendent Darrel Allen. I discovered that he had been prayerfully and effectively applying basic Bible-centered principles of management in his Christian education ministry.

Mr. Allen's relationship with the staff and his leadership of the overall Sunday school ministry encouraged me to look closer at what he was doing. As I studied the material, I desired that its content be shared with students in a Christian education class. The authors responded to my invitation and conducted a seminar which proved inspiring and practical.

Sharing their principles with both professional and lay workers in Christian education seminars, the authors gained acceptance and received requests for more help. Local churches are realizing that not only are their personnel limited, but there are inordinate demands on the time and talent of those who are working. With overloaded schedules, the urgent has replaced the essential and the trivial has supplanted the eternal. Instead of time for prayer and spiritual renewal to sense the Lord's direction in defining God-centered objectives and quality means for carrying them out, there has been daily pressure, frustration, and a keen sense of inadequacy.

Now there is help—practical help, not mere theory. Prayerfully studied and applied, this text could revolutionize your ministry as a vocational church worker or a layman. Figures, charts, and practical exercises included in the text help make new ideas workable. You will be challenged to explore alternatives to your present means of doing the Lord's work. This helpful material is now in your hands for study and implementation. It is with enthusiasm that I recommend it most highly.

Dr. Harold E. Garner
Former Chairman of the C. E. Department
Moody Bible Institute
Director Emeritus, E. T. T. A.

Preface

Three months after beginning my ministry as director of Christian education, the Sunday school superintendent came into my office. Something was on Darrel Allen's mind as he inquired about my plans for the coming year. He seemed concerned that I had not yet prepared plans and began making suggestions for an ambitious program. In frustration I said, "But I don't have time to do the work for such a program."

Calmly he said, "You have been here three months without talking to me once about Sunday school. What do you do?"

"Who does this guy think he is?" I thought. "How dare he talk to a minister like this."

I explained that I worked well over 70 hours a week and was still falling behind. I couldn't add any more work. He replied, "I'm not accusing you of not working. I see your office light on most every night. I know you are working, but what are you doing? Today, for instance, how many hours have you been working?"

"Ten," I answered with the thought, "now I have you." I began listing the things I had done and, with satisfaction, sat back for his response. He added up the jobs and the time I said it took me.

"What did you do with the other five hours?"

Five hours? I couldn't believe it! I added it at least six times, and it always came out the same. I tried to excuse myself by saying, "I must have forgotten something," knowing in my heart that I had forgotten nothing.

Before he left, Darrel challenged me to keep a record of hours worked and jobs accomplished for one week. During that week, I came to work early. I would only stop home for quick meals and then return to the office until late at night. I thought, "I'll show him." Each day the pressure built up as I left my wife, who was expecting our first child, home alone for such long hours.

While work hours increased rapidly, the number of jobs completed grew slowly. At the end of the week I had compiled a very impressive hourly record, but the work accomplished did not come close to matching the time spent. For the first time, I saw the truth of an observation made in an earlier job situation. "He has lots of potential, but no follow-through; lots of ideas, but no organization."

When Darrel came to see me, I was defeated and ready to admit it. He had been aware of my shortcomings and my own oblivion to them. He wanted to help develop my ministry. From his experiences as a public administrator, Darrel wanted to teach me time management, formulation of goals, and how to reach them.

We met on a weekly basis for several months and I began to grasp and apply the management principles he was teaching. Many hours were spent in prayer over the question, "What would God have me do?" For the first time, I began to realize that this was not my ministry. It was God's work, and it should be handled the way He wanted—not by my own personal desires.

Both of us came to a deeper realization that anyone involved in God's service has so much demand upon his time that he dare not waste it. A passage like "Therefore be careful how you walk, not as unwise men, but as wise, making the most of your time, because the days are evil" (Eph. 5:15, 16) began to take on new meaning.

Through development of Ministry By Objectives, God has provided me with tools to determine priorities and to strive with confidence for achievement. We pass these principles on to help alleviate tensions and frustrations felt by lay and vocational leaders in the local church today with the prayer that ministries for our Savior might be strengthened.

Daniel L. Mead

Introduction

While a number of materials provide managment principles and reasons for applying them, very few follow through with actual application. A primary objective of *Ministry By Objectives* is to blend the motivating *whys* with realistic *how to* methods. Practical management activities—prac-tivities—have been integrated in the content with the goal of producing more effective workers for Jesus Christ.

Ministry By Objectives does not attempt to answer *what* questions such as: What should be the objectives for a specific local church program? Instead, MBO stresses *why*, instructs in *how to*, and challenges the worker to prayerfully seek God's will in carrying out his ministry under the Holy Spirit's guidance. Examples are included only for better communication of *how to* techniques. They are models from which to develop your own system.

What answers are avoided because we believe the Christian worker should not let anyone else determine his personal objectives. Each of us is to use the special gifts God has provided. "And since we have gifts that differ according to the grace given to us, *let each exercise them accordingly,*" as Paul states in Romans 12:6.

To obtain the most benefit from this text, we suggest that you first read through it completely to gain insight into the total MBO program and the stewardship cycle. In separate chapters of this text, we will examine each of the cycle elements—appraise the situation, define the work, develop objectives, plan strategy, and review and revise.

Second, set target dates for completing each prac-tivity. Schedule long-range, intermediate, short-range achievement goals with the realization that this experience may necessitate changing some undesirable behavioral patterns.

Satan uses our tendencies to procrastinate and to choose the easy way to discourage completion of the program and realization of its benefits. It will take self-discipline to maintain your schedule in the face of interferences. Prayerfully weigh whether or not a matter is really important enough to disrupt your time schedule.

You are now ready to proceed in developing a more effective work for our Lord Jesus Christ. Learn principles, exercise them, and apply them as God leads. Systematically pray and act upon each prac-tivity in the order given, completing one step before beginning the next. Personal enrichment and growth as well as development of the local church will increase naturally as the priorities of following Christ and glorifying God are maintained.

Appraise the Situation

"But let a man examine himself . . . "

1 Cor. 11:28

As a worker for Jesus Christ, have you given serious thought to how well you are investing God's time? When a frustration-filled day ends in exhaustion, when committee meetings pile up and there seems to be little time for quiet meditation, when things go wrong, how often do you stop to ask God if you're doing what He wants or how effectively you're doing it?

Every believer knows the importance of daily spending time in God's Word and in prayer. Yet, for most of us, personal Bible study and prayer usually get slighted when our schedules are squeezed. Author Charles E. Hummel expresses the situation aptly: "We live in constant tension between the urgent and the important. The problem is that the important task rarely must be done today . . . But the urgent tasks call for instant action—endless demands pressure every hour and day . . . We realize we've become slaves to the tyranny of the urgent." [1]

Redeem the time

God expresses His concern about time and His servants' work achievements in Revelation 22:12: "Behold, I am come quickly, and my reward is with Me, to render to every man according to what he has done." We are in the latter days combating the influences of Satan. We must redeem the time and release ourselves from the tyranny of the urgent.

Good ministry management in the local church is a type of stewardship required by our Lord. Yet, many Christian leaders presently administer tasks and meetings in a tension-filled, pressured environment. Poor stewardship can develop easily. As a result of his experiences and observations, one pastor describes how this negative pattern is created.

> What happens to a minister beleaguered by urgent responsibilities? He takes things as they come, with little or no plan or sense of direction. Since the tasks demand so much of his time, his prayer life is weakened, his study time is abbreviated, his visitation is curtailed, and his family considers him a stranger. He has been cheated of his sources of spiritual power—his means of feeding his own soul and others . . . . In short, he becomes totally consumed with doing the jobs that force themselves upon him and loses sight of the fundamental ministries to which he was called. The urgent has replaced the essential, the trivial has supplanted the eternal.

Jethro must have observed stress and strain in the life of his son-in-law Moses when he exclaimed in Exodus 18:17, 18: "The thing that you are doing is not good. You will surely wear out, both yourself and these people who are with you, for the task is too heavy for you; you cannot do it alone."

Jethro wanted to free Moses from the tyranny of the urgent when he said, "Select out of all the people able men who fear God, men of truth, those who hate dishonest gain; and you shall place these over them, as leaders of thousands, of hundreds, of fifties and of tens. And let them judge the people at all times; and let it be that every major dispute they will bring to you, but every minor dispute they themselves will judge" (Exod. 18:21,22).

Jethro may have been the first management consultant in history. Forty years of wandering in the wilderness was ended nine months after Moses followed his counsel. We should heed how

God used Jethro to provide Moses with good managerial counsel so that Moses' ministry to the people became more effective.

Lead with vision

Christianity today does not need any wilderness wandering or attempts to move the church in divergent directions. The local church needs leaders who have established clearly defined objectives through prayer and the leading of the Holy Spirit and who know exactly what God would have them do. Clear, positive leadership is necessary for the Church of Jesus Christ to prosper.

Evangelicals are beginning to recognize the need to manage more effectively the Lord's work in the local church. Many are grasping that Ministry By Objectives is a Bible-centered means of redeeming the time and becoming more effective in their ministries for Jesus Christ. They recognize that weak organization and poorly defined objectives are causing confusion and crippling the church's effectiveness. Under such conditions, breakdowns in communication and division among God's people in their collective efforts to fulfill the Great Commission are quite likely. Before any improvements or adjustments can be made, it is necessary to appraise the situation. Throughout the text, there are practical management activities—prac-tivities—to complete in order to gain a grasp of the content.

Prac-tivity 1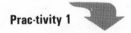

Self examination of our service for the Lord involves considerable prayer and meditation for frank evaluation. In addition, each Christian worker should evaluate his own area of service to determine what the demands are on his time. On pages 14 and 15, time evaluation guides have been prepared for lay workers and pastors to complete so they might gain an accurate picture of how a 168-hour week is used. Similar evaluation guides tailored to the specific duties of other vocational workers also may be prepared. Answer each question on the basis of how actual time was spent rather than how it should have been spent.

LAY WORKER TIME EVALUATION GUIDE

List the average number of hours per week you spend on the following activities:

WORK

Employment (includes housework) . . . . _____

Travel to work (includes travel for shopping) . . . . _____

Routine home maintenance . . . . _____

HOME

Family activities . . . . _____

Family altar. . . . . _____

Family care (doctor, school, travel, other) . . . . _____

RECREATION

Entertainment (includes television) . . . . _____

Fellowship (neighbors, friends, relatives) . . . . _____

Individual activities (golf, sewing, other) . . . . _____

CHURCH

Personal Bible study and prayer . . . . _____

Preparation for serving . . . . _____

Service for the Lord . . . . _____

Worship (Sunday, midweek service, other) . . . . _____

Witness . . . . _____

Total hours _____

Add time for sleeping, eating, personal hygiene . . . . _____

Grand total _____

PASTOR'S TIME EVALUATION GUIDE

List the average number of hours per week you spend on the following activities:

Sermon and Bible study preparation . . . . _____

Sunday school lesson preparation . . . . _____

Actual church services. . . . . _____

Pastoral visitation and evangelism . . . . _____

Church board and committee meetings . . . . _____

Prayer . . . . _____

Systematic study for personal improvement. . . . . _____

Counseling spiritual needs. . . . . _____

Office work, correspondence . . . . _____

Planning and administration . . . . _____

Church-related ministries (funerals, weddings, other). . . _____

Youth involvement (meetings, retreats, other) . . . . _____

Church-related activities(ministers' meetings, Sunday
    school conferences, workshops, other) . . . . _____

Home (see lay worker's sheet for details) . . . . _____

Recreation (see lay worker's sheet for details). . . . . _____

Total hours _____

Add time for sleeping, eating, personal hygiene. . . . . . . _____

Grand total _____

Determine priorities

There are far more demands than time available to achieve them. Each of us is challenged to determine priorities for our lives and service for the Lord in the battle against the tyranny of the urgent. Rather than seek more hours in a day, we must decide upon priorities.

> When we stop to evaluate, we realize that our dilemma goes deeper than shortage of time; it is basically the problem of priorities . . . . not hard work, but doubt and misgiving produce anxiety . . . . We sense uneasily that we may have failed to do the important. The winds of other people's demands have driven us unto a reef of frustration. We confess, quite apart from our sins, "We have left undone those things which we ought to have done; and we have done those things which we ought not have done." [2]

When evaluating how time is spent through prayerfully seeking God's will for your life, priorities may be reassessed according to His perspective.

Prac-tivity 2

After prayerfully examining time demands and priorities for your whole life, take a penetrating look at your performance in serving the Lord at church. Completing the Work Evaluation Chart on page 17 gives insight into how well your work is organized and functioning. Instead of answering *yes* or *no*, give considerable evaluation-thought to each question and express your answer according to the rating (1-5) defined on the chart.

To gain further insight into organization and achievement needs of workers, feedback is needed. The Organization Survey on pages 20 and 21 provides opportunity for honest response by the workers to matters such as: church administration, individual responsibilities, communication, objectives, planning, and supervision. Before completing the survey, pray that God will give the insight needed to evaluate all phases of the work as honestly and objectively as possible.

WORK EVALUATION CHART

Rating system: 1—needs immediate improvement
2—poor, but getting the job done
3—average, but status quo
4—good, above average
5—excellent, needs no further improvement

	Circle one number				
Is your area of service in the church well defined with biblical purposes clearly communicated?	1	2	3	4	5
Does each one involved in your area of service have a written position description from which objectives may be developed?	1	2	3	4	5
Have you clearly outlined the long-range, intermediate, and short-range objectives for your service?	1	2	3	4	5
Has setting objectives been a team effort for the whole church?	1	2	3	4	5
Has a plan been developed that will give workers an action base from which to strive in achieving objectives?	1	2	3	4	5
How well is this written plan for action being executed?	1	2	3	4	5
Have job lists been developed for each worker based upon the plan?	1	2	3	4	5
Is everyone aware of the scheduled activities designed to execute the plan?	1	2	3	4	5
Are workers being challenged to evaluate their own work?	1	2	3	4	5
Has group evaluation been encouraged?	1	2	3	4	5
Is there a leadership review of everyone's work?	1	2	3	4	5
Does this review process lead to a constructive reappraisal of the work and revision to keep it current with new factors?	1	2	3	4	5
Are you at peace with God regarding your effectiveness as a leader for Christ?	1	2	3	4	5
Are His priorities your priorities?	1	2	3	4	5

Plan with prayer

It will be necessary to better manage personal time and to develop priorities in order to begin the MBO program. If there is not adequate time to be effective now, time for developing yourself and your area of service will be hard to find until behavioral changes are made. To overcome this initial barrier, Hummel challenges us to be dependent upon God rather than upon ourselves.

> Prayerful waiting on God is indispensable to effective service. Like the time-out in a football game, it enables us to catch our breath and fix new strategy. As we wait for directions the Lord frees us from the tyranny of the urgent. He shows us the truth about Himself, ourselves, and our tasks. He impresses on our minds the assignments He wants us to undertake. The need itself is not the call; the call must come from the God who knows our limitations. [3]

Prac-tivity 3

Prayerfully review your time evaluation guide to determine priorities in all areas of your life. Then, focus on the time allotted to your area of service for the Lord to determine priorities, schedule activities, and develop work habits. By following the format suggested below, you can begin to organize.

Priorities
- List priorities for your area of service.
- List all known tasks related to these priorities.
- Estimate the time required for each task. If the time demand is too great, re-evaluate your priority list and trim down to meet the available time.

Activities
- Schedule three to six months ahead all known activities related to your tasks. Post your calendar where it is visible.

- Establish a reminder system for completing tasks, and use it regularly. A file with one folder for each month and folders numbered 1-31 can hold notes for scheduled activities. At the start of each new month, place notes in folders for the individual days. Others prefer using a year-long calendar alone. Both systems work if self-discipline is administered. In either case, be sure to program sufficient time to work on developing your MBO program.

Work habits
- Prepare a monthly work plan before the end of each month using your reminder system to prompt inclusion of scheduled tasks for that month.
- Cross jobs off the list as you complete them, making notes which will aid in reviewing your work later and improve your performance the next time a similar task is required.
- Reschedule periodically as you find more or less time available.

A diary such as the one on page 22 will help remind you of the activities to be accomplished during the week.

Now that you have come to a better understanding of the quantity and quality of time used in your ministry, let's move on to the next phase of the stewardship cycle—define the work.

NOTES

1. Charles E. Hummel, *Tyranny of the Urgent* (Downers Grove, IL: InterVarsity Press, 1976), p.5.
2. Hummel, p.4.
3. Ibid.

ORGANIZATION SURVEY

Yes   No

Organization

_____   _____   I understand the organization of the church.
_____   _____   I get direction from only one leader.
_____   _____   If I have a problem, I know who to go to for help.
_____   _____   I understand the purpose and function of each area of service in the church.
_____   _____   We work as a team rather than individuals in my area of service.
_____   _____   Work is distributed fairly in the church.

Position description

_____   _____   I have a written position description.
_____   _____   I have the freedom needed in setting work priorities.
_____   _____   I had input in formulating my job list.
_____   _____   I have enough authority to do a good job.
_____   _____   I would welcome additional responsibility in my work.
_____   _____   I understand my relationships with leaders and workers.

Communication

_____   _____   I feel free to question things the church is doing, particularly in my area of service.
_____   _____   I am satisfied with the openness of communication.
_____   _____   We hold enough meetings to keep me well informed.
_____   _____   I can rely on information I receive from my leader.

Objectives

_____   _____   I know the primary objectives of the church.
_____   _____   My area of service has clearly written long-range objectives.
_____   _____   I have specific, measurable objectives for which I am accountable.
_____   _____   I am involved in the formulation of these objectives.
_____   _____   I feel a part of the objectives of my area of service and those for the church.

Planning

———— I am involved in planning.
———— Work plans are based on annual objectives.
———— I am involved in developing my own work objectives within general objectives of the service area.
———— My job uses most of my skill and experience.
———— The church usually assigns people to jobs best fitted for them.
———— The work is distributed fairly in my area of service.
———— The work plans for the church and my specific area are written and readily available.
———— Policies have been revised to keep pace with changing circumstances.
———— I understand the stated policies that affect me and my area of service.
———— I know where to get written policies of my church.
———— I am involved in decisions which affect me.

Supervision

———— I know what all my job duties are.
———— I have a chance to use creativity in my work.
———— I am encouraged to seek better ways to do my work.
———— I am permitted to manage my time effectively.
———— My leader asks for ideas on job problems.
———— The church gives me enough orientation and training to do my work well.
———— I am able to use the training I receive.
———— The church has a system to meet my training needs.
———— More of our people need leadership training.
———— I would like opportunity to attend refresher training.
———— Leaders have scheduled work for the year to achieve objectives.
———— If I have a problem, I can secure help from my leader.
———— I am often asked my opinion on things which concern me.
———— My leader regularly tells me how I am doing.

WEEKLY CHURCH ACTIVITIES DIARY

Work	Time	Monday Date ___	Tuesday Date ___	Wednesday Date ___	Thursday Date ___	Friday Date ___	Saturday Date ___	Sunday Date ___
Activities								
Letters to write								
Telephone calls								
Personal contacts								

CHAPTER
2

Define the Work

"Make known to them the . . . work they are to do."

Exod. 18:20

At the end of an exasperating day, many Christian workers prayerfully desire that God would send a Jethro to deal with their weaknesses and help them prepare to become more effective agents in today's dark world. God used Jethro, not just for Moses' benefit, but for workers through the ages.

Jethro pointed out to Moses that the task was too heavy for one person, "You cannot do it alone" (Exod. 18:18). He recommended a system of teamwork where the responsibilities were divided among able, God-fearing men. He then advised Moses to outline position descriptions as the first step in resolving the problem.

Clarify expectations

How many times have you been frustrated searching for assistance in youth work, children's church, Sunday school, or other areas? One of the main reasons that few are willing to take a job is because they never know exactly what is expected. A clearly outlined position description allows prospective workers opportunity to know in advance what their responsibilities will be.

Lack of personnel orientation and training also create recruitment problems. How often do we ask someone to take on new responsibility without giving assurance that he will receive the training necessary to do the job adequately? Personnel orientation from the beginning of developing your Ministry By Objectives program is crucial for those persons affected by the objectives set. They should be included in every step of MBO. In addition, a training program is an essential part of the local church organization and should be implemented after the work has been defined, objectives developed, plans formulated, and the team organized.

The local church team must know where they are going, why, what is required, how to work with each other and their leader, and how to evaluate their efforts. Imagine what would happen if a football team appeared on the field, and there were no goalposts or yard lines. What chaos if the quarterback were uncertain which direction to lead the team or what call to make. Similarly in the MBO concept, all workers must know what their roles are and be able to fulfill them.

Lead in discovery

Management in the local church—a combination of faith and reason—is a ministry to people not a manipulation of them. God's Word clearly states the need for leadership and supervision in 1 Peter 5:2,3. "Shepherd the flock of God among you, not under compulsion, but voluntarily, according to the will of God; and not for sordid gain, but with eagerness; not yet as lording it over those allotted to your charge, but proving to be examples to the flock."

To aid in defining the work through position descriptions, areas of service in the local church should be delineated. These areas should further biblical goals of reaching, preaching, teaching, and training others. The purpose of each area should be discovered so that proper emphasis can be placed on the church's reconciliation of men to God through the redemptive work of our Savior Jesus Christ.

Understand position description

In *Administering Christian Education,* R. K. Bower highlights the importance of organization.

When people know what their positions and responsibilities are, then they can begin to coordinate their actions. The prerequisite, however, for good coordination is a structure in which people know what their definite place is in the organization and what their specific duties are. [1]

Both the pastor and lay workers are likely to assume that each person knows his work. Yet, in most cases, for those asked to list responsibilities, authority, and relationships in a job, the written description does not resemble the worker's impressions of the actual job requirements. Such communication breakdowns lead to frustration, confusion, and wasted time and effort.

Much conflict between church boards and pastors would be eliminated if the board would, at the beginning of a pastor's ministry, prepare a position description for him, and the pastor would write his description of board duties. Each should simultaneously write personal descriptions. When expectations are compared, all involved will better understand how to reach agreement so that a final position description acceptable to all concerned can be prepared.

A written position description is the beginning of communicating job expectations. It should not be set aside in a file drawer, but be used as a working document to evaluate and update work on a continuous basis. When clearly defined, a position description helps establish objectives, design plans, perform activities to reach objectives, and review and revamp the work.

Begin organizing

Outlining responsibility and authority allows a worker to carry on his work without asking permission to proceed, a tremendous step forward in redeeming the time. In Exodus 18:23, Jethro reminded Moses of the importance of delegating responsibility and authority when he said, "God so commands you." The Lord knows there is much work to be done. He plans that it be shared with all His servants— "they will bear the burden with you" (Exod. 18:22). In fact, sharing work is a key to success in the local church. Doing otherwise deprives some of the privilege of serving the Lord to the capacity He desires and hinders their spiritual development.

The primary objective for any worker should be to follow in the way God directs. Each can know he is in God's will by experiencing His peace while ministering in the local church. It is worth noting how Exodus 18:23 ends: ". . . and all these people also will go to their place in peace." Unfortunately, lack of solid organization and failure in establishing objectives and plans deprive many workers of that glorious peace with God.

Prac-tivity 4

Indentifying and grouping work to be performed at various positions under each area of service is essential. Purposes for each ministry should be found in God's Word and clearly stated in relation to your local work. Required positions such as committees and boards should be identified. Use the organizational chart on page 27 as a model and prepare your own keeping in mind your church's constitution.

Prac-tivity 5

Formulate a position description for your work which includes:

- the basic function of the position
- the responsibilities and degree of authority to carry them out
- the relationship of this position to immediate leader, boards or committees, or other workers[2]

Involve key personnel in developing their own position descriptions. Such participation will increase accountability for results. On pages 30-32 examples of partial descriptions for lay and vocational workers are provided. The responsibilities, authority, and relationships involved in the positions are examined briefly to provide a pattern for developing your own more fully.

CHURCH ORGANIZATIONAL CHART

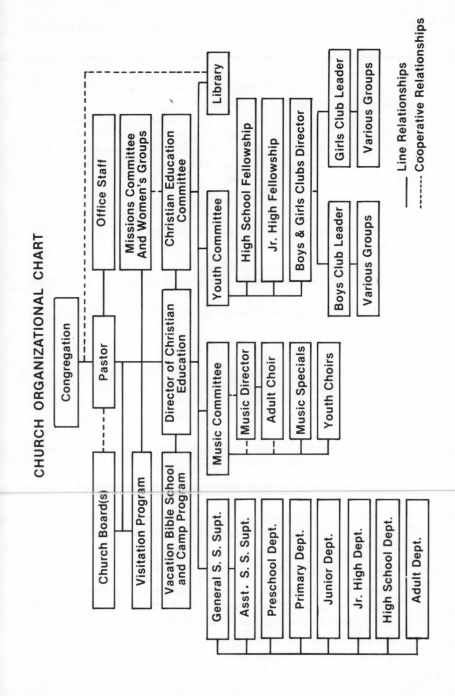

Congregation

Church Board(s)

Pastor

Visitation Program

Office Staff

Missions Committee And Women's Groups

Vacation Bible School and Camp Program

Christian Education Committee

Library

Director of Christian Education

Music Committee

Youth Committee

General S. S. Supt.

Music Director

High School Fellowship

Asst. S. S. Supt.

Adult Choir

Jr. High Fellowship

Preschool Dept.

Music Specials

Boys & Girls Clubs Director

Primary Dept.

Youth Choirs

Boys Club Leader

Girls Club Leader

Junior Dept.

Various Groups

Various Groups

Jr. High Dept.

High School Dept.

Adult Dept.

——— Line Relationships

------ Cooperative Relationships

Invite feedback

Jethro's counsel to Moses and subsequent achievements involved a complete dependence upon successful communication with all God's people. Feedback is vital in effective communication for the developing MBO program. It doesn't happen by chance—it must be planned. Involving workers in the development of their own job descriptions not only provides feedback, but also increases accountability for results.

If the description is found lacking in any area, alterations can be made. In *Function of the Executive*, C. I. Barnard discusses the four conditions to occur simultaneously if alterations are to be accepted as authoritative.

- The person can and does understand the change.
- He believes it is not inconsistent with the purpose of his work.
- He believes it will be compatible with his personal interests as a whole.
- Mentally and physically he is able to comply.[3]

The leader must ensure that those under his direction take mental action on each of these important points and provide feedback. If a response is not motivated during the formulation process, it may appear later in the form of a communication breakdown.

Prac-tivity 6

Creating conditions to further cooperation between workers is essential. As an integral part of God's team in the local church, workers are to reach lost souls and combat the forces of evil. Completing the two activities below will help orient workers to their responsibilities and help unite their efforts.

• Acquaint all workers with the place and importance of their roles. Introduce them to the project of designing a total church MBO program. Be prepared to explain how they can get involved in developing it. A church planning conference or a retreat for key workers may provide the proper setting for further discussion of the program. Sufficient time for effective communication interaction is absolutely essential to initiate a successful MBO program.

• Appraise the needs in training lay workers. Workers should be informed that an MBO training project is anticipated after objectives have been developed and planning accomplished. Organizing their efforts and developing job lists with them will be necessary. Then, use leadership training, teacher training, or other needed types of training to help them fulfill their roles and responsibilities in the ministry.

NOTES

1. Robert K. Bower, *Administering Christian Education* (Grand Rapids: Wm. B. Eerdmans Pub. Co., 1964), p.27.
2. C. L. Bennett, *Manual of Position Descriptions* (New York: American Management Association, 1958).
3. C. I. Barnard, *Function of the Executive* (Cambridge, MA: Harvard University Press, 1964).

Lay Leader Position Description

Sunday School Superintendent

Responsibilities

As Sunday school superintendent, I am to organize the Sunday school to meet departmental, personnel, curriculum, and program needs. The primary responsibility is departmentalization since this provides the framework for an educationally competent school. The needs of every individual from infancy through adulthood should be cared for.

As a leader of leaders, I am to provide guidelines for workers. (Each church must develop its own specifics.)

I must be constantly aware of the curriculum—what is taught, how it is taught, and with what results.

As guardian over the program, I am to keep it biblically oriented and practically balanced with opportunities for instruction, worship, service, and fellowship. I am the mediator between home and church in this cooperative teaching venture.

I am to enlist and utilize an adequate staff. I must outline the responsibilities of associates and see that they are carried out in departmental, personnel, curriculum, and program areas. (These details are left to be completed with regard to your particular situation.)

I am to insure that the quality of every phase of Sunday school work is conducive to spiritual life and growth. Looking for means of improvement, studying the school operations, and evaluating departmental procedures are helpful. By adopting a set of Sunday school standards, I will be better able to measure the progress or problems.

Authority

Being executive head of one of the most important agencies in Christian education, I am to function within the framework of the programs outlined by the church Sunday school board and approved by the Christian education committee.

Relationships

To the pastor—The pastor and I must form a close-knit team. We should consult frequently to discuss policies and plans under consideration.

To the Christian education director and committee—The director of Christian education must work closely with me through the Christian education committee. This committee has oversight of the total educational program of the church and is a policy-building body. I serve as a liason between the committee and the Sunday school staff, interpreting both view points and reporting to each group.

To the assistant superintendent—Much time should be spent with this superintendent-in-training to groom him for the office. There should be a division of labor which keeps in mind his ability to accept responsibility.

To department superintendents—A counseling ministry should be open to each of those key staff members through whom I implement my work.

To the teachers and officers—Leadership for teachers and officers is provided by department superintendents. While these lines of responsibility should never be crossed, recognition of the job and appreciation for services rendered can be expressed.

_____

Sunday school superintendent

_____

Pastor

Vocational Worker Position Description
Director of Christian Education

Responsibilities

As Director of Christian Education, I am expected to participate in daily office devotions and whatever activities are normal for a person serving as a member of the team ministry of this church. Working in close relationship with the pastor, I must assist him in hospital calling and any other pastoral duties requested in the pastor's absence. Finally, I am responsible for coordinating the Christian education ministry.

Authority

Direction will be provided by the pastor and the advisory board with all work being directly supervised by the pastor. Upon approval of proposed programs, I have full authority to carry work to a successful conclusion while maintaining full and complete communication and cooperation with those in authority. Tenure of service is determined by the pastor and the board.

Relationships

To the pastor—The pastor directly supervises my work and assists in developing programs and objectives. I am responsible to keep him informed, being willing to lead as well as be led by his counseling and guidance. While working as a team, he still has higher authority. Full sympathy and loyalty with the pastor, his ministry, and overall program of the church are expected.

To the advisory board—Recognizing that certain programs and policies need board approval and/or that of the church, full cooperation and communication with the board are essential. I serve as an ex-officio member. Tenure of service will be determined by the advisory board and pastor.

To the Christian education committee—This committee is to coordinate and plan a balanced education program and to advance the spiritual well-being of the church. I serve as an ex-officio member.

_____

Director of Christian Education

_____

Pastor

CHAPTER 3

Develop Objectives

"So then do not be foolish, but understand what the will of the Lord is."

Eph. 5:17

Both in mission and means of achieving their missions, John the Baptist and today's church leaders have much in common. John prepared the way for the coming of the Messiah. Our work involves preparation for His imminent return. John had a clearly defined objective and was diligently striving for its achievement. May we make the same claim about our ministry?

Certain special events during the church year, such as the missions conference, Sunday school workshops, and the Christmas program, stimulate cooperation. These occasions require a tremendous group effort to determine objectives, design plans for achievement, recruit personnel, arrange schedules, regulate activities, and meet deadlines. At such times, no one questions the necessity of good ministry management practices. If they are important in the supportive roles of our work, how much more value should be placed upon management practices in fulfilling the higher objectives required of us by the Great Commission. We must concentrate more ministry management effort on effectively working for Jesus Christ.

Direction from the Holy Spirit

Some express concern that Ministry By Objectives might so focus on organizational management effort that the leading of the Holy Spirit will be curtailed. This criticism may be valid only if we do not allow the Holy Spirit to guide the establishment of objectives and if we do not follow His direction in working to accomplish them.

When clearly defined objectives and a plan are lacking, a greater possibility exists for straying from the Lord's methods of achieving His work. Our Lord's admonition that His work be done decently and in order not only glorifies Him, but also helps allay attempts to divert and hinder the work. By helping fulfill His desire for fruitful work in the local church, MBO provides opportunity for pastors and laymen to be more available to the Holy Spirit's leading in their ministries.

Value of objectives

Formulation of specific objectives is the core of Ministry by Objectives. We believe the work of the church is the most important in the world. It cannot be left to chance, but deserves good management care.

God's Word contains many examples of His servants being directed to determine objectives and strive for achievement. The Apostle Paul defined his personal mission when he stated in Philippians 3:14, "I press on toward the goal for the prize of the upward call of God in Christ Jesus." His mission objective is found in Colossians 1:28, 29. "And we proclaim Him, admonishing every man and teaching every man with all wisdom that we may present every man complete in Christ. And for this purpose also I labor, striving according to His power, which mightily works within me." Only after Paul knew specifically where he was going and what he was going to do did he begin his missionary activity. Then, it was with the realization that he was not achieving the work alone. He had a clear sense of his own responsibility and God's direction.

Objectives give direction and purpose. Formulating them is perhaps the most critical activity in the MBO process. Objectives are the basis for determining which activities should be performed and provide criteria for evaluating how well they are being implemented. Without objectives, activities have little meaning. Setting Spirit-led objectives, then, is the key to an effective ministry.

Formulation of objectives

While almost as many approaches to determining objectives are available as individuals setting them, the basic components of an objective remain the same. To develop Spirit-directed objectives, workers, leaders, and pastors must spend much time in prayer asking for the leading of the Holy Spirit and God's continual input in the formulation process.

We suggest two alternative methods for formulating objectives, the top-down and the base-up processes. Precise identification of major areas of service and definition of their purposes are essentials for each method. In addition to individual areas of service, everyone must be acquainted with the total church role and mission.

Failure to define these areas and purposes of service may keep the church moving in so many directions that confusion and lack of achievement result. Keeping in mind the total church ministry, workers and leaders should formulate objectives within the confines of the church's purposes rather than branching out into selected areas of special interest.

Top-down process

The top-down process for formulating objectives originates at the decision-making level. Once policy is determined, it filters down through the total local church structure. The process begins when top level leaders on the church board work with the pastoral staff and the Holy Spirit to determine broad general objectives for the total church program. To illustrate this process, the steps in carrying out an evangelism objective are given on page 36.

Next, middle level leaders in each area of service determine specific objectives for their areas within the confines of the broader general objectives set for the total church by top level leaders.

Finally, service level leaders and workers determine activity-

FORMULATING OBJECTIVES

Top-Down Process

Leadership Levels	Procedure	Example
Top level leaders Pastors Church leadership boards (such as deacons)	Develop broad general objectives for the total church	Evangelism: Church leadership decides that in the next year ____ unsaved individuals in the community should be contacted to offer a gospel witness
Middle level leaders Christian ed committee Missions board Other leaders in defined areas of service	Derive more specific objectives relating to the particular area of service from the general objectives established by top level leaders for the total church	Christian education committee determines to reach youth by starting a community-wide youth club and increasing visitation outreach for Sunday school
Service level leaders & workers Sunday school superintendent Sunday school department superintendents Sunday school teachers Youth club staff Youth sponsors Others	Determine activity-oriented objectives to achieve the specific objectives outlined by middle level leaders which, in turn, will achieve the objectives formulated for the total church	A Sunday school teacher promises to visit the homes of each pupil in the Sunday school class at least once a quarter

oriented objectives for each phase of their organization. These objectives should further accomplishment of the specific objectives outlined by middle level leaders within the framework of objectives determined by top level leaders.

Base-up process

Objectives also may be determined in a reverse process as shown on the chart on page 38. For this base-up procedure to benefit the total church, workers must be totally aware of the organizational structure and purpose of each area of service. If care is not exercised that enough knowledge is gained, mass confusion and branching out may result. But when used properly, this process is advantageous because it promotes an important principle in all MBO practices—*involve all workers at all levels.*

The service level worker begins the process by praying for the Holy Spirit's leading in determining activity-oriented objectives in his area of service. Specific service level objectives are then grouped together by service level leaders to form a collective set of objectives. This process might occur several times within an area, moving from one rank of leader to the next until the general objective has been refined to the highest degree within that area of service.

All phases of an area of service simultaneously formulate specific objectives. Middle level leaders test and refine objectives according to the principles which are discussed below. The composite of these objectives then represents a general objective for an area of service.

Middle level leaders then communicate their objectives to top level leaders. These leaders are responsible for development of total church objectives.

With the base-up process, opportunity for individual leading of the Holy Spirit is enhanced in developing objectives. Individuals do not have to rely solely upon the thinking and directives of others. In addition, when the worker helps design objectives, he is more likely to regard them as personal responsibilities and strive for greater achievement.

FORMULATING OBJECTIVES
Base-Up Process

Leadership Levels	Procedure	Example
Top level leaders Pastors Church leadership boards (such as deacons)	Gather objectives from each area of service and polish them to formulate total church objectives	Sunday school: Church leadership decides that in the coming year overall Sunday school attendance will increase by ____ % and the number daily reading the Bible to ____
Middle level leaders Christian education committee Missions board Others	Test and refine objectives (for each area of service) in accordance with the principles of objectives discussed on page 39	Christian education committee evaluates the degree to which the existing objectives are clearly stated and will result in achievement, with any changes necessary being made
Service level *Overall leaders* Sunday school superintendent Club directors Missions committee officers Others	Solidify objectives determined by various levels in areas of service to reach a general objective	Sunday school superintendent determines total objectives for numerical and Bible reading growth based on each department's desires
Department leaders Department superintendents Club committees Mission workers Youth sponsors Other department leaders	Gather together objectives determined by individual workers and form a collective set of objectives	Sunday school junior department superintendent examines the objectives of each teacher and formulates overall attendance and Bible reading objectives for the department
Workers Sunday school teachers Youth club staff Other workers	Develop activity-oriented objectives in line with the purposes of an area of service and the total church ministry	Teacher determines activities and incentives designed to increase attendance and Bible reading in his class

Principles influencing objectives

In order for objectives to give direction and purpose so that achievement is consistent and balanced, objectives must be stated clearly. Five basic principles must be considered and applied in order to transfer objectives from desired results to achieved ones. The success of MBO techniques corresponds with the degree you understand and apply principles of acceptability, attainability, motivation, measurability, simplicity, and communication.

Acceptability

If an objective is not acceptable, an atmosphere for developing team spirit, mutual supportiveness, and trust are not likely. Instead, suspicion and resentment tend to increase as people fight the objective.

Those who must achieve objectives through the efforts of others should be particularly sensitive to the principle of acceptability when formulating objectives. One simply cannot tell another to do something and expect full-level achievement.

Setting an objective to appease a leader's desires totally violates this principle. Muscle may persuade a person to act when he does not want to, but he doesn't always stay persuaded. It is important to present an objective realistically. Rather than oversell the virtues of an already-prepared objective, it is better to involve others in the formulation process since adding input increases acceptability. The degree of achievement, then, is directly related to how well an objective is received by those doing the work.

Attainability

To be effective, an objective must be attainable within a reasonable period of time. By setting measurable goals, it is possible to determine when and to what degree the objective was achieved.

The principle of attainability strives to foster a balance between formulating realistic objectives and ones that challenge each worker to reach out in achievement for the Lord. Objectives that are too difficult or too simple are often discouraging. Regardless of the degree of difficulty, offer encouragement to workers as they move toward the achievement of objectives.

A leader can be successful in leading others to accept his ambitious objectives, but if he fails to evaluate available manpower, budgeting, or psychological resources properly, the results will be less than satisfactory. They could even hinder future leadership possibilities.

The amount you achieve for the Lord has far more impact on your future than on how well you sell an objective, hence the importance of considering the attainability of an objective. There are times, though, when human reasoning cannot grasp the magnitude of the task God is asking of a person or a church. Particularly at such times, yielding to the Lord's leading and proceeding in faith are necessary.

Easily attainable objectives seem like small tasks, making it easy to overextend one's self with too many objectives at once. When considering your schedule, church work priorities and time with the family should not be compromised or overlooked. Time management and, more important, acceptance of time limitations is critical.

As you get involved in MBO, there is a tendency to program yourself and others beyond the limitations of a 24-hour day, even with easily attainable objectives. At least you believe they are easily attainable, but you failed to accurately evaluate the amount of time available for achievement in the total church program and in individual workers' lives.

Failure to involve workers sufficiently, to obtain adequate feedback, and to evaluate realistically available resources detract from attainability. Care should be exercised that objectives are explained and receive approval because of the Holy Spirit's leading rather than human salesmanship.

Motivation

An objective must be inspirational enough that all personnel want to achieve it. Objectives must be compatible with the interests of the individual as well as meet the needs of the organization. When the development of objectives includes all the team members, this assures individual input and fosters unity.

The extent to which an objective is an effective tool for self-development influences the degree to which the team is motivated. It is important for an individual to establish personal goals within the main objective. In fact, the degree of success in achieving the overall objective and a worker's evaluation of his role in helping reach the objective are directly related to the degree of motivation. To help a worker see his role, a leader should encourage self-evaluation rather than analyze his performance.

While a low-key objective may not get the team moving, an over-ambitious one is likely to disillusion individuals. In the fervor of meeting such a challenge, setting individual goals is often ignored. Then, when it is realized that the effort was not sufficient and no benefits were received, morale can be devastated. Consistent pacing, on the other hand, produces more endurance and more lasting results.

Measurability

When formulating objectives, criteria for periodic measurement must be built-in if success is to be properly evaluated. The principle of measurability builds in a sense of accountability which can greatly increase achievement, particularly if measurement is made on a quarterly basis. Otherwise, no one is going to know if progress is being made.

Simplicity

A simple, clearly stated objective increases the possibility of its effectiveness. A complicated objective, on the other hand, may generate much activity but this does not mean that steps toward achieving the objective were accomplished.

A tremendous obstacle to effectiveness develops when an objective is so complex that God's people wander aimlessly trying to understand what they are to achieve. Nebulous objectives create nebulous results. Therefore, objectives must be kept simple and brief enough to be explained in easily understood words. We may follow the pattern Paul set forth in 1 Corinthians 2:1, "And when I came to you, brethren, I did not come with superiority of speech or of wisdom, proclaiming to you the testimony of God."

In following the principle of simplicity, each leader must take the role of a signal carrier rather than a ball carrier. He needs to know where the goal line is, the simplest route to reaching it, and the best method of communicating this information to team members.

Communication

Progress and problems with an objective must be communicated on a continual basis to all concerned with its achievement. We cannot remain casual and unconcerned about communication since effective use of this principle is critical to a successful MBO program. Few Christians realize that many of the problems within the local church can be traced to communication breakdown. Effective communication is not natural. It takes concerted effort and exercise of proper techniques.

Technical skill is a valuable tool in effective conversation or writing. Yet, it is the desire to serve others and share with them, rather than calling attention to ourselves, that gives a message greater meaning. There is much truth in the saying "If you communicate out of love, you will eventually love to communicate." 1 Corinthians 13:1 also portrays the reverse, "If I speak with the tongues of men and of angels, but do not have love, I have become a noisy gong or a clanging cymbal."

A genuine interest in people and what they say communicates love. Make every effort to listen, disregarding imperfections in style or words. Put away distractions and listen to people as God listens to you.

Prac-tivity 7

Determine whether you will use top-down, base-up, or your own method for formulating objectives. Once a definite system is organized, communicate this method to each level. Allow ample opportunity for feedback to insure that all fully understand the process and their tasks.

Much prayer is needed at all levels. The old nature too easily takes command and turns leadership into a mechanical effort. One has to be on guard at all times. While the church can work endlessly doing things the right way, without the Holy Spirit's leading and provision for the power behind and through the plan, all is vanity.

Using the principles presented in the chapter, you are now ready to outline objectives for each area of service.

Prac·tivity 8

Once objectives have been formulated, classify them as primary and secondary. Scheduling problems then can be avoided when time runs out and priorities must be determined. By identifying the most significant objectives at the time you formulate them, errors of judgment can be minimized at a later date when time does not allow sufficient thought or research.

Next, define long-term, intermediate, and short-term intervals for achievement—in that order—so that dates for completing each phase can be kept in mind. We suggest that during the first year of applying MBO principles and theories you plan no further than one year for long-term, six months for intermediate, and three months for short-term. When you gain experience with the MBO program, this can vary considerably.

Be careful not to develop three separate sets of objectives. Short-range and intermediate objectives are stepping stones for reaching long-range objectives. With objectives in mind and a sensitivity to the Holy Spirit's leading, you are now ready to plan means for achievement.

CHAPTER 4

Plan Strategy

"But let all things be done properly and in an orderly manner."

1 Cor. 14:40

A lack of systematic planning in many local churches implies that the truism "When you fail to plan, you are planning to fail" does not apply to the Lord's work. On the contrary, God expects His workers to plan their work so that they will be able to complete it.

Planning is an integral part of *Ministry By Objectives.* This Spirit-led pre-arrangement of proposed effort must provide adequate detail to reach the stated objectives. Kilinski and Wofford highlight the church's need in *Organization and Leadership in the Local Church.*

> What our churches desperately need today is the thermostat—the instrument that will determine the temperature and the environment. Long-range planning can be that thermostat, for through its effective application a church can act rather than react. As the ability of a congregation to *make* things happen rather than *let* things happen increases, the thermostat of long-range planning will help the leaders anticipate problems and work out solutions before the problems ever occur.[1]

GOAL SETTING AND EVALUATION

Name _____ Period from: _____

to: _____

Interim review / revise target dates: _____

GOALS—be specific	Target date	Evaluation—success or failure? why?

Adapted from Donald P. Smith, *Clergy in the Cross Fire* (Philadelphia: The Westminster Press, 1973), p. 207.

Forecasting

If the present rate and direction of progress continues, where will you be with each major facet of your responsibilities in six months, a year, two years? Evaluation of present work effectiveness is essential before future plans can be projected accurately.

With a better understanding of the present, primary and secondary objectives can be further developed. In forecasting, more details are added to the work done in Prac-tivity 8 so that segments of the objective become activity-oriented goals with specific completion dates.

Defining goals

As objectives are moved from the conceptual stage to goals, achievement can be estimated more accurately. Each goal should be written with specific details, planned on a realistic timetable, and designed to facilitate measurement. A sample Goal Setting and Evaluation form is provided on page 46.

Kilinski and Wofford offer insights into the significant role of goals.

> Goals should be the basis for planning, conducting, and evaluating your church's ministry in a long-range planning project and should be continually displayed through the lines of communication lest the plans become the property of the long-range planning committee, rather than of the church.[2]

Programming

Not only must activity-oriented goals be prepared, a sequence of steps and priorities of effort must be decided. Each step is part of the programming.

A possible sequence and priority rating of general objectives might be: Christian conversion, church membership, Christian worship, Christian knowledge and conviction, Christian attitudes and appreciation, Christian living, and Christian service.

When these general objectives are broken down, a more specific objective for Christian conversion might be "to lead each unbelieving student to experience the forgiving and saving grace of God through Jesus Christ." Steps in this process might include: a personal recognition of inability to live up to God's standard of righteousness and the need for a Savior, a rejection of sin and commitment to Jesus Christ as personal Savior, a growing assurance of the reality of conversion and regard for the Lordship of Jesus Christ.

Scheduling

Set target dates, with the Holy Spirit's help, for beginning and completing each step. Without such structure, objectives will never become more than ideas left to die on the shelf.

Budgeting

It is essential that resources such as funds, time and talent of personnel, and facilities be budgeted before beginning your plan. A church may set a general objective of increasing its outreach in the community. The specific objective for youth ministry is to start a weeknight club to reach boys and girls in the community for Christ. Funding is obviously required, but the proper leadership to develop and carry out the program are more crucial to the achievement of the objective. The importance of leadership cannot be overestimated.

The need for adequate facilities is another consideration in budget planning. With the above-stated objective, a community gym may be desirable in addition to facilities available at church. Any extra equipment required also should be recognized now.

Policies and procedures

Once resources have been included in a budget and plans have been made, must any standardized methods be developed and applied to accomplish an objective? In each area of service, considerable time should be spent defining policies and setting procedures to serve as guidelines.

Policies and procedures should not confine workers, but define boundaries in which individuals may function to achieve their work. Emphasis should be placed upon those areas in which there is room for development rather than stressing restrictions.

To add stability and consistency to the overall church program, policies and procedures should provide answers to questions and problems which occur repeatedly. In addition, leaders
are able to delegate authority through policies and procedures.
Then, by creating an efficient flow of achievement activity, busy
leaders are released from unnecessary burdens and workers are
given the freedom to proceed in fulfilling their tasks.

Planning steps

Even after policies are established, the main responsibility for
planning remains with the leaders. The higher the level of
leadership, the greater the degree of involvement.

At the same time, it is important to stress that inasmuch as
workers were involved in developing objectives, they should
have some input in designing the plan for achieving them. Doing otherwise might jeopardize the continuous flow of worker input at all points in the MBO process. Involvement, on the other
hand, motivates workers to own their tasks and results in a
higher level of achievement. Even more importantly, individuals
have a greater sense of being accountable to the Lord for their
growth and service.

The successful leader uses a systematic approach to planning
which includes the following steps: pray, define goals, gather
facts, analyze data, make decisions, and write plans. With each
of these steps, forecasting, defining goals, programming,
scheduling, budgeting, and determining policies and procedures
should be completed. Prac-tivities for each step in the planning
process are provided.

Pray

Seeking God's leadership and guidance is the foremost consideration of Ministry By Objectives. As we look to our Lord
Jesus Christ, prayer was an important preparation for His
ministry. Mark 1:35 tells how He rose early in the morning to
spend time with God.

Hummel uses this passage to conclude the secret of Jesus'
life and work for God—"He prayerfully waited for His Father's instructions and for the strength to follow them." He elaborates on

the power of prayer. "Jesus' prayerful waiting for God's instructions freed Him from the tyranny of the urgent. It gave Him a sense of direction, set a steady pace, and enabled Him to do every task God assigned." [3]

Prac-tivity 9

Take time to pray for the Lord's leading. James 1:5 promises, "But if any of you lacks wisdom, let him ask of God, who gives to all men generously and without reproach, and it will be given to him."

Now is the time to deal with your doubts and concerns. Allow the Spirit of God to provide the direction and strength needed for achievement. This is a crucial point in the MBO program.

When you feel God's peace about your plans, rejoice in God's direction and strength and proceed in faith. As Psalm 37:5 states, "Commit your way to the Lord, trust also in Him, and He will do it." Belief that a plan won't work after you have committed yourself to His leading in the development of plans denies His promise and inhibits leadership vitality.

Define goals

Following prayer preparation, define a set of specific, attainable, measurable goals. Be sure to write them down.

Prac-tivity 10

To achieve the objectives outlined in Prac-tivity 7, specific goals and target dates for completing them should be set. The Goal Setting and Evaluation form on page 46 provides a helpful guideline.

Gather facts

With your goals in mind, gather all available information regarding manpower needs, availability of personnel, levels of skill required, degree of training necessary before implementation, financial needs, possible sources of funds, facility conditions, alternative means, and time requirements. Each of these factors influences planning.

Prac-tivity 11

Begin obtaining data on all the items mentioned in the above paragraph.

Analyze data

This information must be weighed in light of objectives to be achieved. At this point you are not making decisions on the course of action to be taken, but are analyzing the feasibility of what you want to do and how you want to do it. You may make this a simple or a highly sophisticated process. Be sure to consider: what are the limitations? complications? actions and reactions of people?

Examining the facts helps establish work priorities and promote allocation of funds on the basis of need and priorities. In addition, inspecting information helps insure that jobs are filled, identify training needs, and determine work standards according to the availability of funds and manpower and the skill levels of personnel.

Possibly the most important task to perform after you recruit sufficient personnel and before you begin to execute the plan is training workers. Not only should workers be trained, they should be provided with a set of standards to evaluate progress and to create incentive for doing better work.

Standards help balance the quality, quantity, and frequency of work. When writing standards, be sure to answer questions dealing with these three areas. Consider such questions as: What percentage of accuracy is acceptable? What percentage of growth is satisfactory? What degree of individual involvement is sufficient? The concerns of forecasting, programming, and scheduling also should serve as guidelines for standards.

Prac-tivity 12

Answering the following questions will help you analyze the data that has already been collected:
- What are your work priorities?
- On the basis of need and priorities, how should funds be allocated?
- What are your training needs?
- What standards should be developed?
- Are all parts of the ministry provided for?

Develop job lists

In addition to setting standards, job lists based on specific objectives must be developed for each area of service. This list differs from a position description because it is directly related to achieving specific objectives. It can and should change whenever an objective is reached or revised. A position description, in contrast, outlines broad responsibilities, authority, and relationships.

Through job lists, the degree of effort needed in relation to the number of personnel available and the amount of time they can contribute may be analyzed. Otherwise, a leader could find himself planning more work than can possibly be accomplished. If this occurs, review primary and secondary objectives, the amount of time required for each job, and the frequency of the job to cut back necessary tasks. A review of essentials and a re-evaluation of work priorities in the overall ministry may result in eliminating some specific objectives.

Make decisions

Once all the critical facts are gathered and every aspect of the need for achievement of objectives is analyzed, it is time to arrive at conclusions and decide upon a course of action. If the decision seems rather uncertain or you forecast possible problems, it might be wise to determine alternative plans which could be used at a later date if you have sufficient time. In the meantime, since a decision has been made, proceed in faith with confidence and enthusiasm.

Prac-tivity 13

Draw some conclusions concerning where you will be in six months, a year, and two years with respect to each program being planned. Assuming that the present rate and direction of progress continues, forecast target dates.

Write plans

To be effective, plans should be put in writing. This is visible evidence of your planning effort. In addition, such a document can serve as a reference in each step of the achievement process and be shared with the full church.

The written plan should contain whatever policies and procedures are essential to providing stability, consistency, balance, and efficiency. When such details are given, workers have a helpful vehicle for the accomplishment of specific objectives.

Prac-tivity 14

Now that you have thought through the steps in planning, put them in writing. It is also important to write out job lists for each area of service.

NOTES

1. Kenneth K. Kilinski and Jerry C. Wofford, *Organization and Leadership in the Local Church* (Grand Rapids: Zondervan Pub. House, 1973), pp. 186-187.
2. Kilinski and Wofford, p. 196.
3. Charles E. Hummel, *Tyranny of the Urgent* (Downers Grove, IL: InterVarsity Press, 1976), pp. 8, 9.

Execute the Plan

"But prove yourselves doers of the word, and not merely hearers who delude themselves."

James 1:22

Many workers set aside time for prayerful preparation of objectives. Some go to the extent of designing plans to achieve objectives, but then confine their ministries to paperwork. If the MBO plan is only words filed in a desk drawer, in case someone should inquire about objectives and plans for the coming year, it has little value. Rather, the plan should be closely connected with Spirit-controlled action.

Fear of failure or lack of confidence in your ability to achieve for the Lord all the glorious objectives you desire must be dealt with honestly. Joshua 14 provides an inspiring example of the confidence needed. Joshua stands before the tribes of Israel giving inheritances to those who successfully crossed the River Jordan to the land of milk and honey. The mighty soldier and leader Caleb steps out from the crowd to meet Joshua. He reminds Joshua of their expedition to spy on the land of Canaan and Moses' promise that Caleb would inherit the beautiful mountain Hebron.

". . . I followed the Lord my God fully. So Moses swore on that day, saying, 'Surely the land on which your foot has trodden shall be an inheritance . . .' . . . Now then, give me this hill country . . .

Therefore, Hebron became the inheritance of Caleb . . ." (Josh. 14:8,9,12,14).

Caleb's belief in his ability to accomplish his objective was well-founded. He labored diligently for the Lord forty-five years with this dream in mind. Such measures of confidence and diligence are essential when implementing your MBO plan.

Jesus said in Mark 9:23, "All things are possible to him who believes." The Apostle Paul reinforces the importance of believing in Jesus Christ, the source of his confidence. "I can do all things through Him who strengthens me" (Phil. 4:13).

Involvement

As preparations are completed for achievement of the basic work of the local church, excitement peaks. Not only should each person have a written description of his place in the organization and his individual responsibilities, each should know the church's organizational structure and purposes of each area. Yet involvement should not stop there—each should have helped formulate objectives for the plan of action so they now understand the specific objectives to be achieved and the priority rating of task assignments. In addition, recognizing the importance of setting and meeting target dates for achievement is essential.

The entire congregation—not just workers—should commit themselves to support the program financially, pray for leadership development, and make themselves available for use by God. An awareness of training needs and a willingness to prepare themselves for the work may be required. With all these factors in mind, workers should proceed in a goal-oriented program of accomplishing tasks to the glory of God.

Recruiting, orienting, training, and scheduling the team as well as developing techniques to keep the team's efforts on target are all necessary components in a successful plan. To activate these elements, prac-tivities are included after each section.

Recruiting

Enlisting additional workers to meet needs indentified in the planning stage is the most critical phase in executing the plan.

CHRISTIAN SERVICE SURVEY

Date _____

Name _____ Home phone _____

Address _____ Zip _____

Occupation _____ Work phone _____

Indicate choice(s) of service with a number in front of a program interest. No. 1 represents first choice, no. 2 second, and so forth. Place the same number by position and age group.

Program	Position	Age group
____Sunday school	____Teacher	____Cradle roll
____Children's church	____Sponsor	____Nursery (ages 2, 3)
____Training hour	____Club director	____Beginners (ages 4, 5)
____Boys/girls clubs	____Helper	____Primary (gr. 1-3)
____Vacation Bible school	____Secretary	____Junior (gr. 4-6)
____Library	____Storyteller	____Junior high (gr. 7-8)
____Camp	____Song leader	____High school (gr. 9-12)
____Youth group	____Pianist	____College
	____Crafts	____Adults
	____Other_____	____Other_____

Check (✓) other ways you desire to serve

Music
____Sing
____Direct
____Play_____

Missions
____Write missionaries
____Gospel team

Visitation
____Home visits
____Telephone
____Read to shut-ins

Hospitality at home
____Meals
____Overnight guests
____Youth meetings
____Adult activities
____Swimming pool available

Audiovisuals
____Projection work
____Tape duplicating
____Radio ministry

Publicity
____Graphics
____Journalism
____Bulletin board preparation

Office work
____Stenography
____Record keeping
____Mailing

Athletics
____Recreation director
____Coach_____

Building maintenance
____Carpentry
____Electrical
____Painting
____Plumbing
____Lawn care
____Masonry

Miscellaneous
____Usher
____Transportation
____Arrange flowers
____Cook
____Nursery attendant
____Public speaker
____Social committee
____Other_____

Hobbies/Special interests _____

Rather than enlist personnel and then design work to meet their talents, identify the job and recruit individuals to meet the needs of that position. Churches must learn to draw upon their untapped reservoir of workers.

> The primary task . . . is to do careful research on people who have identified themselves to the body of believers, to know each individual in the congregation well enough to recognize his spiritual gift, to learn of his past experience, and to be aware of his abilities and training. The items necessary for conducting this research are (1) an up-to-date list of the membership, (2) a membership profile questionnaire, (3) a program for obtaining the information, and (4) a system for keeping it available and up-to-date.[1]

The Christian Service Survey on page 57 is a possible means of gaining membership profile information mentioned in item (2) above before recruitment begins.

Prac-tivity 15

Using your organizational chart, list each position required for the area of service in which you are involved. Indicate where there is a vacancy. Then, keeping in mind Prac-tivity 12, finalize job lists for each position listed on your chart.

If your church does not have a current membership profile, try involving the church board and pastoral staff in conducting a service survey. A form similar to the one on page 57 will provide helpful information for consideration when recruiting personnel to fill vacant positions.

After discovering capable individuals through the membership profile information, leaders should give each prospective worker a position description and a specific job list. Ask him to pray about accepting the position. Be sure to follow up and obtain a decision.

Orienting

Once the team is together, newly recruited personnel should be given a full MBO orientation similar to that suggested in Prac-tivity 6 on page 28. It is critical to stimulate enthusiasm in new workers to own the objectives and work plans. Often, using other lay workers in the process of acquainting new members with the goals, plans, and sense of accomplishment of different service areas helps build team spirit.

The entire team should be given a set of plans which include specific job lists for each individual. Further, they should be made aware of the decisions resulting from prac-tivities and be reminded of the four conditions listed on page 28 for a person to accept alterations as authoritative.

Prac-tivity 16

Provide all workers with a set of the plans and a job list of the specific tasks to be accomplished within a set period of time, such as three, six, or twelve months. Each should be given a Goal Setting and Evaluation form similar to that on page 46 for writing personal objectives. This list should collectively meet the specific objectives outlined in the plan and the general objectives of the full church. Actually, this step finalizes the formulating of objectives that was begun in Prac-tivity 7.

If a Performance Covenant such as the example on pages 67 and 68 is going to be used in Prac-tivity 20, its meaning should be explained so that prayer preparation can begin now.

Training

With specific training needs defined, objectives set for training workers, and means to accomplish the task designed, now provide a training course. This opportunity to equip workers to do the jobs the Lord has placed in their hands cannot be accomplished within a short time span. Training is a continuous experience.

Short-range, intermediate, and long-range goals identified in the plan should be clearly outlined and agreed upon for the personal development of each worker. We recommend that the Evangelical Teacher Training Association's training courses be fully implemented in your program. Evangelical Leadership Preparation (E.L.P.) books are also helpful.

Prac-tivity 17

Develop a calendar of available training courses and enlist personnel to begin training. E.T.T.A. representatives are willing to provide guidance in setting up a continuing training program.

Scheduling

Prac-tivity 3 on page 18 provided scheduling methods to increase organization. Yet, at such an early stage, it was like picking up a handful of rocks and throwing them in the direction you believed the target was located, hoping that wherever it was you might hit it. Now in addition to planning tools, objectives provide a visible target. Therefore, scheduling takes on fresh significance in executing your plan.

With this new perspective, individuals must estimate the time required for each task on the job list. Where time conflicts, they should select priorities. Which are the most important tasks? Which have the most pressing deadlines? Which can wait? Posting a calendar and/or tickler file with a three- to six-month planning schedule is helpful.

Prac-tivity 18

Have each individual estimate the time required for the tasks on his job list and select priorities. A calendar and/or tickler file with at least three to six months scheduled ahead should be posted by each person.

Lay workers should prepare a monthly work plan before the end of each month and, with the help of a reminder system, schedule tasks for the coming month. Vocational workers should prepare weekly work plans.

As tasks are finished, cross them off your list. Make notes so that later when reviewing your work you can improve the performance on a similar task. Time should also be taken to reschedule periodically as you find your plans changing.

Supervision

To make sure that work the leader has assigned is carried out in accordance with the plan, staff meetings, appraisal sessions, and on-the-field review of work can be held. Designing control techniques to facilitate continuous evaluation is the last but most important step in executing the plan. More details will be provided in the next chapter.

Supervision is not a new concept in church work. Sunday school workers have long recognized the need for standards and a system for reporting information to assist in continuous evaluation. Consequently, numerous report systems have developed for the Sunday school ministry.

It is important that leaders and lay workers develop a simple, workable system which will provide information on a regular basis. The need exists in all areas of service.

Report systems

Utilizing report forms not only keeps the team on target, it also serves as an excellent communication vehicle to keep everyone informed of work progress—a key element in the motivation of workers. With the feedback of such reports, workers may transform planned objectives to recorded achievements on their own.

In conjunction with the position description on page 32, we have developed a report form for vocational workers on page 62. On this Monthly Ministry Report, hours on the job and the number attending are vital statistics. Such figures increase awareness of

MONTHLY MINISTRY REPORT

A record of hours worked and persons reached

_____, Assistant to Pastor   Month _____

Day of Month	Bible Study/ Prayer	Assist Pastor	Counsel		Chil-dren's Church		Sunday School		Youth Meet-ings		Bus Ministry	Visi-tation		Others
			hrs.	no.	hrs.	no.	hrs.	no.	hrs.	no.		hrs.	no.	
1														
2														
3														
4														
5														
6														
7														
8														
9														
10														
11														
12														
13														
14														
15														
16														
17														
18														
19														
20														
21														
22														
23														
24														
25														
26														
27														
28														
29														
30														
31														
Totals														
% of total ministry														

Total days worked _____ Total hrs. worked _____ Avg. hrs. wkly. _____

MONTHLY REPORT FOR GROUP ACTIVITY LEADERS

Group _____ Month covered _____
Completed by _____ Date _____

Please submit your report to the church office as soon as possible each month.

Comments (use other side for further space)

1. What % of enrollment attended the meetings? (Divide average attendance by number enrolled.) _____ %

2. What was the average attendance at this month's meetings? _____

3. Was there any response, such as salvation or dedication?

4. What was the average score for any quiz or tests given? _____

5. Evaluate achievement of this month's meetings towards reaching objectives. (check one)
   ____1 Needs immediate improvement
   ____2 Poor, but getting the job done
   ____3 Average, but status quo
   ____4 Good, above average
   ____5 Excellent, reaching objectives

6. Using the above scale, evaluate the following: 1 2 3 4 5

   Participation   _ _ _ _ _
   Attitudes   _ _ _ _ _
   Lesson materials   _ _ _ _ _
   Planned activities   _ _ _ _ _

7. What could you have done to make improvements?

8. What can be done to make programs more effective?

9. Did you plan any extra activities for your group this month?

10. Could you have used more help? In what ways? By whom?

where priorities are being placed and whether or not these fit in with stated objectives. If greater detail is desired than can be contained on this chart, daily and weekly reports can be made.

A sample report form designed for lay worker use is provided on page 63. Because of such diversity in lay work, we offer the following principles to keep in mind when designing your own forms.

- Keep forms as simple as possible.
- Limit questions on the form to ten.
- Design questions to obtain exact information concerning: frequency (of participation), quantity (of persons attending), quality (of learning), and evaluation (of achievement).

Prac-tivity 19

The Monthly Ministry Report on page 62 illustrates the type of form that a vocational worker might wish to prepare for his work. Using this as a general format, individualize the categories listed to fit your particular circumstances. When appropriate, be sure to keep track of attendance as well as hours worked.

For lay workers, the Monthly Report for Group Activity Leaders on page 63 provides helpful guidelines. Be sure to obtain exact information as simply as possible.

Performance covenant

The personal involvement of individual workers and the importance of owning every aspect of service are stressed in all phases of the MBO process. Despite the efforts of leaders to involve workers in seeking God's will in each step of MBO, the danger is still present that a worker feels separate from the process. A written commitment, such as a performance covenant, facilitates a final action where the worker accepts the process as a part of himself and something personal between himself and God.

A performance covenant can be employed to achieve supervision as well as secure and remind of commitment. Because the covenant is a very personal matter, leaders must give each individual opportunity to follow the leading of the Holy Spirit in his life and service. A worker should never be manipulated or forced into a performance covenant. Instead, the leader should motivate, counsel, guide, and encourage the individual to continue a relationship of full commitment and dependence upon his Lord in fulfilling his responsibilities.

To develop a performance covenant, use the position description, job list, and goal setting evaluation forms previously considered to show the stated general, specific, and personal objectives for each worker and leader. The covenant consolidates these three documents and formalizes an agreement, a written commitment, between an individual and his Savior. If the covenant does not seem necessary, rely upon a position description, job list, and goal setting and evaluation form.

Prac-tivity 20

Design techniques to facilitate supervision. If you decide to use the performance covenant system, this may initially be confined to leaders or it may be channeled down through the church organization and involve many covenants. When considering the following steps in developing a covenant, remember the leader's role is as a helper, counselor, and coach.

Performance covenant steps

• Adequate time must be devoted to spiritual preparation. Seek the Father's instructions and pray for strength to follow them. A dependency upon God rather than striking out on one's own direction and upon his own strength is essential.

• In outline format, list each facet of responsibilities identified in your position description.

• Within the outline, express in narrative form your personal objectives for each facet. Ultimately, these should lead to the achievement of specific objectives for your area of service.

• Under each facet include specific tasks contained in your job list.

• Keeping in mind that this is a covenant between an individual and God, the leader reviews the first draft and provides feedback concerning the effectiveness of the covenant in achieving the specific objectives of that area of service.

• This feedback is prayerfully considered as the worker finalizes his covenant vows.

NOTES

1. Kenneth K. Kilinski and Jerry C. Wofford, *Organization and Leadership in the Local Church* (Grand Rapids: Zondervan Pub. House, 1973), p. 56.

SUNDAY SCHOOL SUPERINTENDENT
PERFORMANCE COVENANT

For the Sunday school to be an effective educational agency, I must commit myself to work toward its becoming better organized. To meet this objective in the coming year, I intend to do the following.

• A continuous evaluation is necessary of how well Sunday school *departments* are functioning within the existing framework. The middle school 6-8 grade unit seems to have weakened the junior department. Division of grades will have to be decided.

• *Personnel* work needs considerable attention. I intend to establish a full roster of substitute teachers to cover for absent teachers; visit teachers and encourage them to increase concern for visiting students and to develop closer student-teacher relationships; and to encourage teachers to renew interest in continuing their training, arrange training courses, and provide worker's meetings to assist in motivating and educating teachers to do their work. I will seek more outside speakers with expertise in special areas where we must improve such as evangelism and church-family relations.

• *Curriculum* appraisal is important because a variety of publishing houses are used. A systematic approach to total Bible coverage is essential.

• *Program* concerns should center on openings in each department. In addition to evaluation of new curriculum materials, there needs to be a concerted effort to secure parental cooperation.

Administration

• *Departmental* tasks include working with the Christian education committee to develop dynamic Sunday school department leaders to replace those serving presently. A better Sunday school welcoming procedure should be developed.

• Besides tasks listed in the position description for *personnel,* I want to develop a Sunday school handbook, encourage teachers to be available for pre-class time with students, and promote an intensive visitation program.

- *Program* emphasis will be placed on developing better church community communication regarding the importance of the Sunday school. Through the church paper and other means, Sunday school attendance will be promoted.
- *Supervision* improvements to add to those already listed include: evaluation of techniques used in the Sunday school, monthly appraisal of missionary Sunday promotion in each department, encouragement of missions projects, and assistance to department superintendents in promoting attendance at workshops and motivating teachers to a higher level of commitment.

(Any other matters can be included here. Attaching a Goal Setting and Evaluation form would also be helpful.)

———————————————————
Sunday school superintendent

———————————————————
Date

Review and Revise

"This I pray . . . abound still more and more in real knowledge and all discernment, so that you may approve the things that are excellent."

Phil. 1:9, 10

To persevere toward the achievement of Spirit-directed objectives demands a reviewing system which communicates progress on a regular basis. Use of a continuous review system signals problem areas which can be corrected before they become critical. Evaluation must be as constant as achievement activity itself. Otherwise, the alternative is crisis-oriented review when things begin to fall apart.

When MBO is working properly, review is primarily self-appraisal. The worker detects any deviations from or failures to meet his performance convenant or stated goals. He acknowledges these and seeks help from the leader to correct them.

Changes in the situation, resources available, shifting of priorities, or any other change in circumstances may cause failure. Then, the leader and worker revise the existing performance covenant or goals in line with the new realities. As soon as problems or failures surface, they are to be confronted openly, frankly, realistically—and resolved—rather than ignored, camouflaged, or blamed on others.

Leadership concepts

The leader must fully accept his role as a guide and not overstep his power by trying to dictate or manipulate. This could damage the overall MBO program and diffuse the ownership that has been carefully cultivated at each step of the process.

A democratic form of leadership provides the best relationship between workers and the leader. Questions should be asked to evaluate leadership effectiveness: Does the worker feel he has self-control? Or is control being imposed on him by the leader? Can the worker see the results of his work? Or is he dependent upon the leader to tell him how well he is doing?

Too often we have drawn an imaginary curtain between what the worker does and the results he accomplishes so that he has only a vague notion of achievement. Educators confirm that leaders should inform workers concerning their job effectiveness. What happens all too often is that the leader observes the results and remarks, "You did OK, but I'm sure you can do better if you work a little harder with a bit more consecration." Rather than providing a system for the worker to judge his own performance, the leader has offered a vague interpretation of results.

When a worker does not know what he should be doing to improve, he does not know where he is making mistakes or how much he should improve. Consequently, it is extremely difficult to make corrective adjustments in his behavior.

Leaders should encourage the worker to take ownership of his position in the church and its tasks. When full responsibility for his actions is gained, performance can be measured directly rather than filtered through the leader. The leader is to work in the background serving as a resource person and counselor, assisting the worker in accomplishing his job more effectively.

Private review

The need for a worker to see the results of his work is demonstrated in the following illustration.

An archer stands poised to shoot at a target. He fires and sees his arrow pierce the outer circle at the top right. He aims again; the arrow hits farther to the left and lower. His third arrow strikes the center of the target. What has happened? . . .

First, we have a person who is motivated to persevere, who knows his responsibilities, and has the ability to perform well . . .

Second, we have a target—a goal that is clearly visible and unambiguous in its design, conveying to the archer the goal that he is seeking . . .

Finally, we have feedback. The archer can see how well he is doing. He knows the direction and degree of his error.[1]

Each worker should use the Goal Setting and Evaluation form and/or his performance covenant as his target. Work activity is the bow and arrow. The evaluation section of the goal setting form on page 46 and the Self-Evaluation Work Sheet on pages 72-74 will give him the vision necessary to see how close he is coming to the center of the target.

Leaders should encourage workers to schedule evaluation on no less than an every-six-month's basis. Meanwhile, a leader should help workers develop an attitude of continuous evaluation and problem solving. Conflicts should be met head-on for immediate resolution rather than waiting until an evaluation date to resolve a known problem.

Prac-tivity 21

Be sure to fill in the evaluation section of your Goal Setting and Evaluation form on page 46 on the date that you already determined to discover how close activities are bringing you to your objectives. After this is finished, complete the Self-Evaluation Work Sheet on pages 72-74.

Group review

Rather than an alternative to private review, group review is the next step in an orderly process of reviewing work progress. In

SELF-EVALUATION WORK SHEET

Name_____Date_____

MY SPECIFIC WORK RESPONSIBILITY

1. What goals have been set for me in my present responsibilities?

To what extent has each goal been achieved?*

	1	2	3	4	5	6	Comments

2. What activities are connected with my present work? (Don't forget routine duties.)

To what extent has each activity contributed to reaching goals?*

	1	2	3	4	5	6

3. Which of the activities in no. 2 have I found the most satisfying? Which have given me a sense of achievement? (List the three most important and define the satisfying factors.)

4. What have been the principal frustrations or obstacles in my service?

5. What sense of calling do I have in my work? How does it compare with an earlier sense of calling?

6. The degree to which I feel I possess the quality described in each phase below is indicated by the rating checked in the appropriate column opposite it. (Leave blank if not applicable.)

---

*1 Outstanding   3 Good   5 Fair
2 Very good   4 Satisfactory   6 Poor

(continued)

Self-Evaluation Work Sheet (continued)

Qualities	1	2	3	4	5	6*	Examples
Work							
a. Use my skills							
b. Develop new skills							
c. Carry out my responsibilities							
d. Initiate appropriate activities without being asked							
e. Set work priorities and keep them							
f. Suggest creative ideas							
g. Accept ideas of others							
Teamwork							
h. Provide leadership when needed							
i. Cooperate with other leaders							
j. Encourage leadership							
Relationships							
k. Relate well to most people							
l. Quickly sense how others feel							
m. Express my positions diplomatically but clearly							
n. Listen to others, whether or not I agree with them							
o. Act as peacemaker							

---

*1 Outstanding   3 Good   5 Fair

2 Very good   4 Satisfactory   6 Poor

(continued)

Self-Evaluation Work Sheet (continued)

Qualities	1	2	3	4	5	6*	Examples
Personality							
p. Usually cheerful, seldom depressed							
q. Persevere against obstacles							
r. Control my temper							
s. Constructive and helpful in my criticism of others							
t. Maintain poise in embarrassing situations							
u. Free from anxiety or nervousness							
v. Accept criticism and praise graciously							

7. What are my strong points?
8. What are my weak points?
9. What difficulties have I had in relations with members of my church?
10. How have I dealt with them?
11. To what extent do my present responsibilities make use of my abilities, interests, training, and experience? (Be specific as to which are not now being adequately used.)
12. In the light of my achievements, strengths, and limitations, what would an ideal job be like?
13. What alternative types or places of work might I consider if I did not continue where I am now?
14. To what extent have I been growing personally (skills) and spiritually?
15. What resources have contributed to my growth?
16. What reading has influenced my thinking most in the past year?
17. How do I feel about the trends and policies of the church where I serve?

---

*1 Outstanding   3 Good   5 Fair
2 Very good   4 Satisfactory   6 Poor

Adapted from Donald P. Smith, *Clergy in the Cross Fire* (Philadelphia: The Westminster Press, 1973), pp. 208-213.

Prac-tivity 7, objectives were identified for each area of service. Each worker has already had opportunity to review his work. With this knowledge, he is now equipped to interact on a group level and gain insight into how well the team is working together towards achieving the objectives of that area of service.

The leader responsible for group review needs to further an atmosphere of ease and team spirit for the evaluation process to be effective. Workers must not feel they are being interrogated. Instead, everyone should feel free to comment and make suggestions without fear or anxiety. Uninhibited interaction is the key to successful group review.

Focus on group goals, not individual ones. The same Goal Setting and Evaluation form can be used to list group objectives as well as individual or general ones.

Throughout the evaluation process, the review purpose must be kept clearly in mind. It helps determine whether you are on target. If not, corrective action can be taken to reach the objective. When such measures are not sufficient, revisions will be necessary to meet the new circumstances. Without careful review and evaluation, these weaknesses might not have been discovered and ineffectual activity would have been allowed to continue.

All review of work, whether done privately or in a group, should be positive and aimed toward future achievement rather than dwelling upon past failures. All too often reviews center upon a balance of complimenting the worker for good points and chastising him for weaknesses. Bower points out the positive scope of evaluation.

It is not the responsibility of the evaluator to judge or recommend dismissal; rather, it is to encourage, to guide, and to help every member of the church in his God-given ministry, however large or small. It is that of studying personalities with their related skills and then seeking to place them where they can function most effectively for God.[2]

Prac-tivity 22

On a date that has already been determined, use the Goal Set-

ting and Evaluation form to evaluate how closely the activities of
your group are meeting stated objectives.

Leadership review

One would think that after a private review encouraged and
guided by a leader and a group review directed by a leader that
there would be no need for further action. However, a leader-
worker session can be vital in keeping work moving in a positive
direction.

Leadership review is a pivotal point in the MBO process. Communication at this level is a necessary final step before an endeavor
can be revised. Often, the worker is not aware of the full impact a
change can have on the whole MBO program. He needs consulta-
tion to discover further insights into the problem or to gain additional resources (financial, personnel, equipment . . .) which the
leader is best equipped to provide.

Once a new perspective is gained, the worker does not always
have the authority to revise an objective. Consequently, if a
change is deemed necessary after evaluation in the leadership
review, it is the leader's task to make any changes in his scope of
authority and suggest any others to the next higher appropriate
authority.

Leadership review does not replace daily supervision. A
periodic review of performance summarizes a person's work over
an extended period of time. Since the time between reviews may
be long, the leader must be constantly alert to the needs of those
under his charge through weekly observations of work behavior.
Instruction, training, meetings, and week-to-week counsel concerning performance should help raise the level of achievement as
well as the peace and accomplishment felt by the worker.

Prac-tivity 23

Leaders should interact not only with their groups but also with
each individual involved. Such review helps determine progress
and evaluate what changes are necessary in light of overall objectives. These changes should then be initiated as fully as possible.

Revise

The three levels of review should result in a continual updating of the MBO program. Necessary revisions should be initiated whenever a problem surfaces.

The purpose of this Review and Revise step is not to execute all the revisions detected in the review process. It is a time set aside at least once a year to make those necessary program revisions which will insure that changes made during the year's activities are compatible with the general objectives and programs of the total church.

Actually, this segment links up with the appraisal segment which began the stewardship cycle. Work is then redefined through prayer and the leading of the Holy Spirit. New objectives are determined each year as the previous year's plans are updated and related to new circumstances and changing times. Applying the stewardship cycle completely at this point will further the achievement effort for workers in the local church.

Prac-tivity 24

Set aside time at least once a year to make necessary overall program revisions to insure that changes made during the review processes are compatible with the general objectives and total church plan.

NOTES

1. Kenneth K. Kilinski and Jerry C. Wofford, *Organization and Leadership in the Local Church* (Grand Rapids: Zondervan Pub. House, 1973), p. 182.
2. Robert K. Bower, *Administering Christian Education* (Grand Rapids: Wm. B. Eerdmans Pub. Co., 1964), p. 132.

A FINAL WORD

"If you do this thing . . . then you will be able to endure . . . "
Exod. 18:23

Jethro found Moses frustrated and overworked when trying to give needed direction to God's people. In the midst of his frustration, Moses was presented with the prospect of peace. What a difference it would make if each church leader could come to the end of a year with a real sense of peace rather than frustration.

God has never desired that His people wander in the wilderness. He has always wanted them to arrive at the Promised Land. Unfortunately, too many of us are in the wilderness and cannot even see the shores of our destination in today's local church programs.

Following Jethro's counsel, Moses roused the children of Israel. Together they moved out in the same direction with the same objective to reach the Promised Land. The end result: leaders of the Hebrew nation were able to endure and lead the people to their place in peace.